From a New Forest Inclosure

The First Two Years

GW00417635

By

Ian Thew

Published by Burley Rails Publishing
Burley Rails Cottage BH24 4HT

ISBN 978-0-9570835-0-9

Ian Thew

Born in Southampton, Ian and his siblings were brought, throughout their childhood, into the New Forest to walk and enjoy the open space. Although, initially, he spent his adult life living and working away from the Forest he was always keen on the countryside and country sports, especially fishing and shooting. He returned whenever he could to the Forest until, eventually, he settled down in Burley with his late wife, Diane. In 1994 they moved to the remote Burley Rails Cottage which, originally built as a woodman's cottage and sold by the Forestry Commission in the 1960's, is a unique place in which to live.

Ian's knowledge of the forest is genuine and he is respected for his considerate and well researched articles which are published in national and international magazines.

These booklets have been produced with the encouragement of readers who wished to refer to a particular article which had been lost in a discarded magazine and at the suggestion of those who wanted friends, relatives and visitors in general to understand the Forest and its ways. So whether a Villager, Visitor, Tourist, or Grockle, whatever your guise, we hope these snippets will help you to understand what is so very special about this wonderful place.

After an extended holiday to America in 2004, where I visited amazing places like the Grand canyon, Bryce canyon and Monument Valley, I was returning home along my access track when I realised just how special and unique, in the great scheme of things, is this New Forest of ours and I decided that the time had come to put pen to paper to share with others some of the experiences I enjoyed, on a daily basis. My first article was accepted by the editor of the village magazine and I was immediately encouraged to share more of my observations. And so began the series of short articles entitled, originally, 'From the Enclosure'

Ian Thew

July

When you are privileged, as I am, to live in the heart of a New Forest enclosure, the urge to travel to far off places is seldom felt. However, after many years of being contented with my lot and never leaving The Forest for more than the odd day or two, I was persuaded to take a three week holiday, and a thoroughly enjoyable time I had too.

It was apparent, on my return, that my reluctance to leave the Forest for any prolonged period of time, has made me less aware of just how quickly it changes at this time of the year. During my relatively short absence the transformation has been quite dramatic. The oaks and the beeches have pushed forth their fresh green leaves and their increased weight has lowered the branches to form a canopy over the previously bare driveway. Whilst alongside the track, the bracken fronds have leapt up at an alarming rate and spread their mantles to hide the drab winter floor.

The house sitters have kindly cut the grass in my absence, but sadly an incredible number of weeds have invaded and engulfed the kitchen garden and I don't look forward to the effort that will be required to evict them.

All over the house the climbing plants are running amok and really should be cut-back, but several species of birds have taken up residence and consequently this job will have to wait. A pair of Pied Wagtails are busy nesting in the Golden Ivy close to the bathroom window and their close cousins the Grey Wagtails are secretly nesting elsewhere on the house. They can be seen in their bright yellow vests bobbing on the ridge tiles, their beaks crammed with food, but they are reluctant to reveal the location of their brood and refuse to go near their nest while I'm watching. Several pairs of blackbirds are busily searching the lawns and flower borders for tasty worms and may well be on their second or even third brood by now. Any good intentions I may have had with regard to pruning the climbers have been quashed by a Spotted Flycatcher that has built a nest on the extension ladder, which is hanging in the tractor shed, and I'm grateful to it for providing a further excuse for me to postpone an unpleasant task.   The four species of Tits that normally swarm over the various feeders and fat balls are conspicuous by their absence. They too are feeding their huge broods and have forsaken my easy pickings and are busily foraging in the Forest for juicy caterpillars which are the preferred diet of their offspring. They have been replaced however, by quarrelsome Greenfinches and the more colourful but equally aggressive Siskins, but both give way to the enumerable Great Spotted Wood peckers and their red-crested young that regularly swoop down and hammer away at the peanuts.

Fallow Buck in velvet

It's not only the birds and plants that have been busy, the Fallow Bucks have cast their antlers and already sport the velvet knobs that will rapidly develop into magnificent heads, and at the same time the common coloured variety are changing their coats into the rich chestnut pelage with its cream coloured spots, that is so typical of the species.

A walk through Windy Wood reveals a most unexpected but welcome find, several of the fallen Beeches are covered in layers of delicious Oyster mushrooms and these, together with an even bigger surprise in the shape of two early but nice-sized Ceps or Penny Buns that I espied under the bracken, will make a tasty wild mushroom risotto for supper.

I enjoyed my travels in foreign parts and no doubt will do it again if prompted, but is marvellous to be back in this lovely Forest of ours, especially at this vibrant time of the year.

August

We will all remember the early days of July as cold and wet and totally untypical of the season, and I must confess that like so many other wimps I turned on the central heating on more than one evening. But we tend to remember the unpleasant things in life and in actual fact it was cold only for a relatively short time, it was certainly wet, but generally warm, and these weather conditions usually encourage some species of fungi to make an appearance. I reckoned it was time to have a serious foray for some of the most eye-catching and gastronomically pleasing of all the free food that is available to us in this most magnificent of forests.

I decided to disregard the many jobs that required attention and, in case I should change my mind, I quickly took my basket, stick and knife, together with my motley crew of dogs and off we went into the nearby wood to see what we could find. Two hours later I returned with a marvellous haul of Chantrelle, Hedgehogs, Ceps and Oyster mushrooms.

Chanterelle

Mushroom hunting is a truly rewarding hobby and where better to indulge oneself than in the New Forest where the many and varied habitats support enumerable species of fungi, some edible and some definitely not. You may wish to stick to the mundane selection of mushroom varieties that are available in the supermarkets or you may choose to get off your bottom and go onto the Forest and collect the much tastier wild fungi that are there for the taking. However, if you should decide to become a mushroom gatherer then there are certain rules that must be followed.

There may be up to 12,000 species of fungi in this country, many of which are edible, most are not worthy of the table and a few are,

Cep, Porcini or Penny Bun

without doubt, deadly. These fungi take many forms and they play a vital part in nature, they help to break down dead animals and plants thereby creating the food needed by living plants and animals. The fruiting bodies provide food and shelter for many insects and animals and some yield the drugs and antibiotics that have saved so many lives. So we must, for many reasons, proceed with caution.

The best way by far to begin to learn about fungi is be shown by someone that knows the subject, so tag along with any experienced mycologist if you can, or enrol in one of the Forestry Commission's guided mushroom walks where you will be shown many fungi by an expert.

A good reference book is essential and the one that is regarded as the mushroom gatherers Bible is "Mushrooms and other fungi of Great Britain and Europe" by Roger Phillips and published by Pan Books. For further information and recipes try "A passion for mushrooms" by Antonio Carluccio and "The mushroom feast" by Jane Grigson.

Some parts of the Forest are inviolate and fungi collecting in these areas is not permitted. There will usually be a sign to this effect but if you are in any doubt then consult your local Keeper. Pick only enough fungi for your own consumption; the recommended limit is no more than 1.5 kg per visit. You will need a light stick for probing under the bracken and leaf litter together with a sharp knife to cut off your prizes at ground level. By cutting the fungus you will avoid contaminating with soil the gills and pores of the other mushrooms in your basket and you will not damage the delicate, underground mycelium. Always gather your mushrooms in a wicker basket, don't carry them in a plastic bag, they will sweat and lose condition quite rapidly.

Before you start make sure that you can identify the mushrooms that you are after. The four species mentioned above would be good starters for the beginner; they are all common in the forest and are easily identified. Always take a reference book with you and never pick any fungus that you cannot recognise and never put an unknown fungus in the basket with those that you intend to eat. Make sure that you can identify the poisonous species as well as the edible ones and do not disturb mushrooms that you do not intend to pick; they play an important parting the general ecology of the forest.

Finally, I cannot emphasise enough how careful you have to be with mushrooms. A lack of caution could lead to serious gastric disorder and in some cases an unpleasant death. The golden rule is that if you are the slightest unsure of a mushroom leave it alone, do not pick it and certainly do not eat it.

Good hunting

Male Great Spotted Woodpecker

September

Some like it hot and some don't. I must confess that I don't, and as I write this in early August the sun is blazing down from a cloudless sky and the temperature must be in the eighties, as far as I am concerned, it's an ideal time to sit in a cool study to scribble-out some more ramblings.

It's interesting, however, to observe the birds and the animals and to note how they individually handle the heat. My cocker spaniel bitch and the little Jack Russell are both sun worshipers, they are lying on their backs in the full sun with their paws in the air, shamelessly displaying their anatomy for all to see. Not so the retriever, his thick black coat absorbs the heat and he has sensibly scraped a cool hollow in the soil under a dense bush, similarly the venerable old Labradation is stretched out on a wooden bench in the cool of the Pyracanthus arbour. Needless to say both cats are in a deep sleep in the extreme temperature of the conservatory, and there they will stay until hunger arouses them.

Some birds love the heat, not half an hour ago there was a cock blackbird on the sloping roof of the dog house. His body was flattened against the scorching tiles and both wings were spread out to their full extent either side of him. His bright yellow beak was wide open in the extreme temperature; he seemed to be in a trance and was quite oblivious to his surroundings. Quite definitely he was sunbathing and seemed to be enjoying every minute of it. Several of the enumerable rooks that feed on the old air field at Stoney Cross were also soaking-up the sun this morning. How comical they looked as I drove by, standing beside the road, their black bodies bent to one side with one wing fanned out and touching the ground and the other opened fully and pointing to the sky. They too were open-beaked and obviously enjoying themselves.

The sight of those dozy rooks brought to mind a tame rook that used to frequent my house long ago before I moved into the Forest. He would strut into the living room of my little cottage on a cold day and head for the fire, any cats or dogs that happened to be stretched out in front of the fire would be evicted by a sharp prod from his vicious beak and they would hastily head for a safer if colder corner. He would then adopt the same position as the rooks on the airfield and he would stay there for several minutes until the heat became unbearable, at which point he would dash outside or find a cooler spot. A few minutes later he would return and repeat the process until he'd had enough. He also had the most marvellous party trick, he had a passion for cigarettes and he would swoop down on any unsuspecting smoker, and having stolen their lit cigarette from mouth or fingers he would land on the ground in front of them and vigorously preen his feathers with the hot tip. I don't know why he did this but I can only guess that it was a way of ridding his plumage of unwanted vermin.

We had a visit yesterday afternoon from another chap who didn't seem to mind the heat. I was sitting in the conservatory with my big cat Boris asleep beside me.

The door to the patio was opened wide and I had fitted a wooden slatted frame into the opening to prevent the entry of unwanted wet dogs, fresh from a cooling dip in the pond. It was a very hot and sultry afternoon; nothing stirred, only the occasional feathered visitor to the nut feeders. The dogs were nowhere to be seen, no doubt the long walk we had just taken had left them tired and they were probably asleep in their respective chosen locations on such a day. I too was becoming sleepy and the crossword clues in my newspaper were beginning to merge into one another as my eyes started to close. I shook my head and tried to refocus on the puzzle and it was then that my eyes caught a movement on the patio. I could not believe what I saw; a half-grown dog fox had brazenly walked onto the patio and was busily sniffing the paving under the table. I didn't move a muscle and much to my amazement he came right up to the frame and stuck his muzzle through a gap in the wooden slats, and a pair of bright eyes peered at me through the gap above. I was enthralled; he was no more than eight feet from me, but what to do? If I moved a muscle he would surely be off. Suddenly Boris the cat, who I thought was asleep, flew from the settee and spitting fiercely he swiped the fox's muzzle with extended claws. Poor old Charlie didn't hang around, he was off in a flash of red and was last seen wriggling through the stock proof fence and into the forest. And the cat? Well, after a few minutes grooming and rearranging his ruffled fur he jumped back onto the settee and promptly went to sleep as if nothing had happened. Stay cool!

Boris

October

Yesterday was the first day of September and it proved to be a warm sunny day without a drop of rain, unlike the August bank holiday weekend and the preceding week when we wondered if the rain would ever stop! Many campers have packed-up and gone home earlier than planned and a distraught farmer declared on breakfast TV that this was the worst harvest in years. The crops have been flattened and soaked by the heavy rain and increased oil prices mean more costs to the poor farmers who are forced to use corn dryers as they struggle to salvage something from their fields. I was thinking about these unfortunates as I walked the dogs in the early morning sunshine, but not for long. My thoughts were distracted by the glistening, dew-covered cobwebs that festooned the bracken, gorse and grasses all around, a lovely sight to behold and a sure sign that autumn is just around the corner. Autumn is that time of year when I think about gathering-in my own harvest. I refer of course to all the wild produce that is there for everyone to collect, should they so wish, and what a bumper crop we are going to have. The changeable weather that has caused so much grief to the holidaymakers and farmers has encouraged a wealth of wild goodies and, provided we don't experience any untoward weather conditions there will be plenty for both man and beast. The Fungi harvest is already underway with an abundance of Ceps along the forest rides and enumerable Chantrelle and Hedgehog mushrooms peeping through the leaf litter of the Forests floor. Oyster mushrooms swarm all over the fallen beech trees in Windy Wood and Field Mushrooms are winking brightly in the road-side verges and Forest lawns. The oak tree beyond my study window is smothered with fresh green acorns and no doubt the pigs will soon be turned-out to gobble-up this bonanza before the ponies eat too many. The beech boughs already sagging with their prolific leaf growth are now straining under the added weight of an incredible crop of beech mast. The hairy husks are opening in the sunshine to reveal two three-cornered nuts which will drop to the ground and provide food for a huge variety of birds and animals. The beech mast together with the acorns will attract massive numbers of

Wood Pigeons, the blue hordes will come from far and near to gorge themselves on these delicacies and no doubt some of them, in turn, will end up in my freezer.

The hawthorn beside the garage is also straining under its load of

Oyster Mushrooms

bright red haws; these tiny pithy fruits can be made into wine or jelly but I don't bother, I enjoy watching the birds that flock in numbers to the tree to eat the insipid berries.

The rowan trees are similarly ladened with bunches of red berries and are readily stripped of their fruit by many species of birds.

A few hazel trees grow beside Blackensford brook and they have, to my knowledge rarely produced more than the occasional nut. Go and have a look at them, this year they are covered in nuts and these will provide food for the wood mice and squirrels during the lean winter months, and I'll probably have a few for myself. Come up the track from the brook and you will notice that the sweet chestnuts are not to be outdone by the hazels; their prickly green nut cases are prolific and swelling rapidly with the promise of a good harvest of the sweet glossy brown nuts, in the late autumn.

The hollies behind the deer sanctuary have more berries than I ever recall seeing, they're green at the moment and not too obvious among the equally green foliage, but soon they will turn into that gorgeous, waxy red that typifies this most festive of trees, and when they do they will be a feast for the eyes. Likewise the crab apples on Backley plain are heavy with fruit and some crab apple jelly may be produced before Christmas. Like the hazel nuts these tiny apples provide food for birds and animals well into the winter months.

Some of our older villagers will tell you that this natural bounty is the harbinger of a cold and hard winter; I'm not so sure, but let's wait and see.

It would be impossible to think of autumn fruits without giving consideration to two of my favourites, the blackberry and the sloe. Like everything else this year, both are in abundance and very early. A dear old friend picked pounds of juicy blackberries just

Holly

beyond Ashurst at the beginning of august! As for the sloes, every bush is full of the small, bitter, plum like fruits, but there they will remain until the first frost has come and gone and then they will be carefully picked from the thorny branches and converted into that most welcome winter warmer.... Sloe gin.

Cheers!

November

I was standing at the gate for no reason that I can recall, when I was hailed by a man who was hurrying down the track in my direction.

"I've just seen a big herd of stags" he panted, without the courtesy of a 'good morning' or 'hello'.

"Good morning". I replied "They would almost certainly be Fallow bucks, not stags."

"Oh no, I'm not having that" he snapped, "I know they're stags 'cos they've got big horns" and without further ado he continued on his way muttering under his breath about 'know-alls'.

I was sorry that my response had irked him but his comments did not surprise me. There seems to be a good deal of uncertainty among some of us when it comes to the recognition of and the terminology related to the species of deer that live in the Forest. So, at the risk of sounding like a 'Know-all' let's take the opportunity to highlight some of their distinguishing features and at the same time try to unravel their mysterious nomenclature.

There are six recognised species of wild deer in Great Britain. Of these six species only two are true natives; the others have either been introduced or have escaped from private zoos or deer parks. One of the six is a non resident of the New Forest, and unless you have a penchant for skulking around in the reed beds of the great east- coast river estuaries and fens, then you are unlikely to see the Chinese Water deer in the wild.

Of the Forest residents the Red deer is the largest wild mammal in Great Britain and is a true native. It can be confused, however, with its close relative, a Japanese import called the Sika.   The males of both species are known as stags and the females as hinds, whilst their offspring are called calves. During part of the year Red and Sika stags carry large, branching, pointed antlers --- not horns, please! But how to tell them apart? The Red is a much bigger animal and as the name implies it sports a rich, red coat in the summer, the Sika's coat however, is covered in creamy spots arranged in horizontal rows. The Red has large lozenge-shaped ears whilst the Sika's ears are shorter with broad lobes. Because most people's view of Forest deer is usually the back end of the animal as it disappears at a rate of knots over the horizon or into the undergrowth, it is useful to be able to recognise each species from behind. The Red sports a natty yellow rump which extends above a relatively short tail but the Sika is much more spectacular it has a pure white rump patch that can be fanned-out when the animal is alarmed. Its tail is short but has a black line down the centre During the mating season or rut as it is known the Red stags can be heard roaring, a sound not unlike that of a cow, The Sika stags whistle at this time of year, which can be quite unnerving when heard for the first time, in a wood, as darkness falls.

It is thought that early in the middle-ages the Normans introduced the Fallow to this country. It is heavier than the Sika and is the most numerous deer in the Forest. It is best known in its summer coat of rich chestnut covered in sparse creamy spots, but this species can also come in melanistic (black), white, or menil (a light beige colour). The fallow male is known as a buck and mature animals carry large palmate antlers. During the rut, they can be heard 'groaning' or 'belching' on their stands. The female Fallow is a doe and her offspring are called fawns.

Red Deer

Fallow deer have a long active tail with a black/brown stripe down the middle and all but the white varieties have a black inverted horse-shoe shaped mark on their rump.

We have two more species of deer in the Forest, the Roe and the Muntjac; both are considerably smaller than those we have already looked at. In both the males are referred to as bucks whilst the females are does, their off spring are called kids.

The Roe is a native deer and it is leggy and graceful, the Muntjac, however is an Asiatic escapee that is extending its territory dramatically. It is an ugly little beast, smaller than the Roe and with a hunched posture.

The Roe is identified by its bright red summer coat and large black-rimmed mobile ears. The buck is easily recognised in the season by his short, sharp, pronged antlers. Roe deer are the only species without a tail in the U.K but like the Sika they can both fan out their lemon coloured rump patches when alarmed. Both buck and doe utter a single 'barh' if suspicious and if trapped or extremely frightened can emit a terrible scream.

You are more likely to hear the Muntjac or 'barking deer' as it is also known; both sexes will bark continually —not dissimilar to a terrier, when they suspect danger. The summer coat is chestnut brown with white underpants and their long tails are white underneath and ginger on top.

When alarmed and in flight, the tail is held erect like a white flag and the small white rump patch is exposed. Both bucks and does have large canine teeth or tusks and the bucks in season carry short inward curved antlers.

Well there you are, a brief resume of the deer of the New forest, I hope it has been of some use, but if not --- oh deer!

December

Now, I must bring your attention to a more serious subject. I've had my wrist slapped, my knuckles have been rapped, I almost had my bottom smacked---but not quite, thank goodness. I have been charged by a representative of no less an austere body as the Forestry Commission of the grievous offence of the use of the word 'Enclosure'; he says I should be writing 'Inclosure' and who am I to argue with such a venerable organisation? I defer to local knowledge and the more observant of you will have already noticed the change in the heading of this months scribble.

But was I wrong to use 'Enclosure'?

"Yes" I hear you say---but only because you're all in possession of Ordnance Survey maps of the Forest and as that equally respected body repeatedly uses the word Inclosure then surely, Inclosure it must be.

I wasn't so sure, so I referred to that definitive of tomes, The Oxford English Dictionary, and as the letter 'E' comes before 'I' in the alphabet, I looked-up the word Enclosure first, and I quote: "the action of enclosing, especially the enclosing of waste or common land", so far so good. Next, the word Inclosure, and once again I quote: "Variant of Enclosure". Interesting! But it didn't help to explain why, in the Forest, the preferred use is Inclosure and not Enclosure? I decided to use my limited home library to undertake further investigation.

I discovered that in his book 'Portrait of The New Forest' Brian Vessey-Fitzgerald writes about Enclosures when referring to the 1483 Encoppicement Act. Heywood Sumner, a most prolific and knowledgeable writer and resident of the Forest shows a preference for Enclosure and under "Places of Interest" he boldly heads one location as "Backley Enclosure."

Even the Forestry Commission in it's guide entitled 'Explore the New Forest' refers to Enclosable land and also to Charles II, who Enclosed New Park. On the other hand, in 1899 C. J. Cornish wrote of "some 20,000 acres Inclosed since the year 1700", and in the countryside writers bible 'The Language of Field Sports' by C. E. Hare, a 'Park' is said to consist of "Vert, Venison and

Inclosure". Finally, in her book 'Records of Burley', Miss F. Hardcastle a much respected historian and past resident of the village refers to a copy of Richardson, King and Drivers map of 1787 which clearly names both Burley Enclosure and Sandys Enclosure. Whilst the Ordnance Survey map of 1872 which is also shown in the same book lists Oakley Inclosure.

Now there's food for thought, personally I'm none the wiser but I'm sure there will be someone out there who is!

Originally, the word 'Enclose' meant to shut-up. So without further ado I will now enclose but not before I wish you all a very merry Christmas.

January

I had been away for a week or more and had lost track of the natural cycle of the Forest. I was keen to take a walk and so with dogs and binoculars I set off on an early December morning and headed in the direction of Backley Plain. The weather was unseasonably mild, almost spring-like I thought and as if to reinforce my reflection a Great Spotted Woodpecker began prematurely drumming on a nearby tree. All around me as I walked were signs of the passing fungi harvest and I wondered if there would still be anything worth eating. On a whim and without much hope of success I headed through the Inclosure towards a location that had proved to be very fruitful during the recent season. I have to tell you that I was pleasantly surprised to find a few golden-yellow chanterelle peeping coyly over the fallen leaves in my favourite ditch, whilst lower down by the little excuse for a stream, huge hedgehog fungi were roaming in great profusion out of the ditches and over the forest floor. A little further on and I came to a fallen beech and there clinging in tiers were a family of silver-grey oyster mushrooms. I would have to return later with the knife and basket and take advantage of this late bounty.

The Forest floor was deep in dry, brittle leaves and as we progressed through the trees hundreds of blue-grey wood pigeons clattered away in alarm as we approached. Their great numbers formed a dark cloud as they disappeared in the direction of Bratley Wood. They had come from all over the country to gorge themselves on our abundant beech and acorn harvest; I do not recall having seen such numbers in recent years. Similarly, on Sandy Ridge vast flocks of redwings twittered overhead; these pretty Scandinavian thrushes have shunned the cold of their native countries to glean our winter harvest.

As I head for home I am aware that the Forest has undergone a dramatic change. The trees that a few days ago were a blaze of stunning reds and yellows are now bare of leaves, but to compensate for the loss they have laid a thick carpet on the forest floor. I don't like to see the trees so bare but I am glad when, at last, they are all down.

Have you ever taken time to consider leaves? They start their lives in the spring as coy little things that peep shyly from their buds. Slowly they unfold into soft, gentle, green fellows and, as the year progresses they mature into thoughtful creatures that provide shade from the sun and shelter from the thundery showers. But look out when the autumn is upon us, for it is then that they undergo a change and emerge as nasty little devils full of evil intent. They leap from the trees en-mass, hell-bent on mayhem; they block gutters, drains and culverts, causing flooding to properties, highways and the Forest; they unite in thick soggy layers on tracks and driveways and stubbornly resist all efforts to evict them. Finally, if left to their own devices and as a parting insult they decompose into a thick, sticky, brown sludge.

Wet leaves will stowaway on the soles of shoes or on dogs paws and once indoors they will jump-ship and cling stubbornly to any floor surface. But it's when they are dry and brittle that they're at their most mischievous. They steal into homes through any open window and laze around on carpets and rugs. They chuckle to each other as they disappear up the vacuum hose knowing that they have pre-arranged to congregate at the bend in the tube to cause an obstruction. Watch out as you open the kitchen door, for sometimes they are in collusion with the wind and they will rush between your feet, laughing as they skid across the tiles, to finally break ranks and disperse to all corners of the room. I'm not insensitive, but there is a certain amount of pleasure in watching the smoke curl from a bonfire of leaves on an autumnal afternoon!

I'd better stop talking about leaves before I'm accused of rustling!

Have a happy and prosperous New Year.

March

A long walk through the Forest on Christmas morning has always been compulsory in the Inclosure, (perhaps that's why I rarely have house-guests at Christmas) and this year was no exception. Off we went with the motley crew of dogs and headed in the direction of Blackensford brook, which meanders just east of the cottage at the bottom of Woolfield hill. The track was very muddy from the pre-Christmas rain and the short walk to the brook was, in part, more of a slither and slide than a walk. However, the going became easier as we turned northward and followed the river upstream. I hadn't been down here for a few weeks and whilst the little brook chuckled over the gravel shallows between the deeper, tannin darkened pools, the flotsam and debris that festooned the banks above the water indicated a much higher river, and not too long ago either. The flatcoated retriever, typical of his breed was in the river, whilst the other dogs were mooching on either bank. A splashing in the river, just at the point where the water ran over a shallow bar into the deeper water downstream, caught my eye. The aforementioned water-dog noticed it at the same time and with lunging bounds it ploughed through the river intent on urgent investigation. As he approached the spot, a large dorsal fin broke through the surface followed by a broad back and furiously thrashing tail.

"Leave it", I yelled. I know a trout when I see one, and this one was big. The dog did as he was told and halted in a spray of water- - and the fish? It disappeared. I climbed into the stream and walked through the shallow water and the dog and I, side by side, peered into the brown depths of the deep pool. In this little stream it's possible to find small fish such as brown trout, bullheads and minnows, but this, compared to these little chaps, was a veritable leviathan. There was no doubt in my mind that our monster was a sea trout and that it was running up stream to spawn, but I was very surprised to spot it so late in the season; the previously mentioned rainfall must have lifted the river high enough to encourage it to move on. With the heel of my Wellington boot I scraped a channel through the fine gravel in the shallow bar. I had no sooner stopped my excavation when the fish, with a flick of its tail shot through the channel between my feet and took refuge in the next deep pool. It was about two feet long and my estimate of its weight would be about six pounds. I watched it swim away upstream and marvelled at the tenacity and determination of these lovely migratory fish.

It felt compulsory now to continue along the river in the hope that more trout might be spotted—fat chance with four dogs sniffing and lolloping in the water. About half a mile on a flash of white under the conifers on our left took my attention away from the stream. A white fallow buck stood motionless in the trees and as I watched him I realised that he was not alone. These deer have a habit of standing quite still when a possible threat comes near, and I counted a further thirty or more common coloured bucks all standing quite still and staring in our direction. Then, without any obvious reason one of the group broke ranks and started to run. That did it; the whole herd disappeared in their stiff-legged, bouncing, ground-eating, run, which is known as 'pronking'. Fallow are the most common species of the Forest deer and there are many around us, but it's always a pleasure to see them.

With the fallow gone we took a turn around Bratley wood and eventually came to the gravel track on Sandy Ridge and there, across the track, was a most unexpected bonus and a marvellous Christmas present. A herd of red deer, and when I say a herd, I mean a herd! I've seen the odd stag and small groups of hinds out here before now, but this was something else. I counted five stags of varying ages, two of which carried magnificent 'heads' and accompanying them were twenty-nine hinds. They were about forty yards away and seemed as interested in us as we were in them. Like the earlier fallow they all stared in our direction, heads raised as they sniffed the air, and then casually one of the masters turned away and walked off over the ridge and into Backley Bottom. The rest of the group in turn, followed him at a leisurely pace. We watched them disappear and headed towards home along the gravel track.

We reached the enclosure fence at Blackensford hill. This spot has always been known to me as 'Gods Gate' and for many years I accepted the name without question, until one day I noticed under

27

the top rail of the little wicket a carved inscription which reads 'ALL THIS BEAUTY IS OF GOD'. I have asked many knowledgeable people if they could enlighten me as to its origin; so far no one has been able to offer an answer. Someone, long ago, painstakingly carved this statement and didn't feel the need to sign it. I will probably never know who the carver was but I agree wholeheartedly with him or her—this Forest of ours is certainly beautiful and we must thank whichever God we worship, for it.

Then home to Christmas dinner and what do you suppose we had, trout maybe, or was it venison?

God's Gate

April

Thirty minutes ago when I sat down at my desk to write, it was a beautiful sunny morning and now, the sky has blackened; the Douglas firs across the clearing are swaying violently in the wind and huge hail stones are pounding on the window of my study. It has, so far, been an unusual autumn and winter and it had been my intention to pooh- pooh the old adage that a bumper autumns harvest is the harbinger of a hard winter. The winter so far has been unseasonably mild, but it takes only a short sharp hail shower such as the one I have just witnessed to remind us that February and March can harbour some very severe weather. I'll reserve, if you don't mind, any comments on old country sayings until April, let's say, just to be on the safe side.

I hope, however, that the weather doesn't do anything too drastic. There are many early birds who will get more than the worms! As I write, a great tit is flying back and forth from the forest to a nest box on the wall above my study window. I've no doubt it has every intention of taking up residence on my house but it's certainly very early! The hordes of pigeons that have invaded the Forest are in the main, still with us. Many will return to whence they came before long, but some of the more hopeful resident birds have been observed carrying early nest-building twigs in their beaks. Great spotted woodpeckers abound in this part of the Forest and at the moment I awake to their drumming on most mornings; indeed, any bright sunny morning for the last few weeks has been heralded by their drumming, something not usually heard until the spring. The cock blackbirds with their bright yellow beaks have been sparring in the borders and there are at least two new nests close to the house.

The squirrel population has exploded and even greater numbers can be expected as ardent males chase their intendeds through the bare canopy at eye-defying speeds.

But mild winters have their downside. Ticks, those most despicable of insects which would normally disappear when the cooler months are upon us, have been found on the dogs and cats throughout the autumn and winter. Garden weeds that are knocked back during periods of hard weather seem to thrive and lawns that are too wet to cut keep growing. Butterfly and bumble bees, lulled into a false sense of security by the mild weather, are aroused too early from their hibernation. And as for me, I miss the cold frosty mornings and the clear sharp air. You can't beat a crisp morning for a walk in this magnificent Forest.

Found any frog spawn yet?

Douglas Fir

May

We returned, recently, from a long walk to discover two nice ladies waiting at my gate with a dog. They had found it wandering on its own and thought it might be one of mine, but it wasn't. A telephone call to the number on the dogs disc and a thoughtful friend who took the dog to his own house (which is far easier to locate than mine) and dog and owner were soon reunited.

The incident made me think and it occurred to me that the number of lost dogs that I have encountered in the past is not that great. I have lost count, however, of the number of lost people that have rolled up to my gate. More often than not there will be two of them and they will ask if I can direct them to 'the car park'. When I ask them in return which car park in particular, they will look at each other in amazement and almost without fail, one of them will utter those immortal words.

'Is there more than one, then?'

There will then follow a short quiz. By asking them questions such as:- Is there a toilet in the car park, or an ice cream van, or was it near the deer sanctuary etc., I can usually, by a process of elimination, steer them in the right direction.

Last year the dogs were letting me know that there was someone at the gate. I opened it to find a young lad in a uniform. He was in khaki shorts and shirt and he had a kerchief around his neck. He called me Sir and produced a map... he was lost. I took the map and was about to show him where my house was when he politely stopped me and putting a whistle to his lips he blew a long blast. He was looking down the grass ride to our right so I turned to see what he was up to. I was amazed to see, trotting towards us, seven or eight more lads in similar attire. Even more amazing was the man who brought up the rear; he too was dressed in the same uniform, but he was also festooned in maps and compasses which flapped against his chest and legs as he bounded toward me. I struggled to keep a straight face, he was a big man and stretched his clothes to the limit, and he reminded me of a caricature of a scoutmaster that I had once seen. After closer examination I came to the conclusion that he was carrying just about every navigational aid, know to mankind.....how could he be lost? The lad called him 'Skip' and explained that I could help. He took my advice politely and without question and they all thanked me in turn as they set off on their way. As the last lad went past I asked him who they were. He told me they were Air Cadets and that they were on a navigation course. My reply to him was that I would certainly not be flying with them in the future!

Most people are polite and usually relieved to be helped but there has only ever been one person who didn't get my help. Once again the dogs warned me of interlopers and as I approached the gate I heard the babble of several voices. There was one voice that dominated the others and the owner of that voice glared at me as if I shouldn't be there, when I stepped through the gate. I asked if they were lost and could I help? He referred to me as 'my good man' and told me in no uncertain terms that he had never ever been lost in his lifetime. He nodded towards the house and told me with a smug look that it was Railway Cottage. I replied in the negative and he gave me a hard stare and said that I was wrong! I couldn't believe my ears. I pointed to the house name on the fence beside me. He looked at it and once again told me I was mistaken. I didn't know who he was, but I wasn't going to put up with this arrogant individual who was telling me that I didn't know the name of my own house! I asked him if he was absolutely sure that he had never ever been lost before. He confirmed, in no uncertain terms, that he hadn't.

'Well congratulations' I said as I turned to leave him to it. 'You are now!'

Now its time I got lost too.

July

I think it's now safe to say that we've well and truly dismissed that old myth that says a bumper autumn harvest will be the harbinger of a long hard winter. The Forest harvest last autumn was one of the most prolific and diversified that I can remember and did we have a tough winter? No, not at all. In fact the weather has been so unseasonably mild that we are currently witnessing an explosion in the rabbit population throughout the area. It seems that the warm weather and abundance of food had encouraged the little devils to start breeding much earlier in the year than usual. We all know that rabbits have a reputation for being prolific producers but I must admit that I wasn't prepared for the sight that met my eyes when I responded recently to a call from a desperate lady, who was at her wits end with the rapid destruction of her garden, by these buck-toothed vandals. There were rabbits in the garden, rabbits in the driveway, rabbits in her paddocks...rabbits everywhere of all shapes and sizes and the damage to the garden alone, was unforgivable.

Rabbits are not the only creatures who have taken advantage of the warmer winter. On more than one occasion this year I've spotted grass snakes swimming in the garden pond. They were obviously hunting for frogs or newts to ease their hibernation induced hunger, but they had emerged much earlier than normal.

Judging by the number of road-kills observed throughout the winter, the badger population seems to have taken little or no winter hibernation. They will, under normal conditions and when cold weather makes food scarce, retire to a warm underground chamber lined with fermenting leaves and there they will sleep away the winter. During spells of warmer weather they will often emerge to see what can be picked up. I have spotted dead badgers on the road side throughout most of the winter months and the entrance holes to my resident badger sets have been, more often than not, left open, indicating a decided reluctance, or need, to hibernate.

The bird nesting season is well underway and as well as the regular garden inhabitants like the blackbirds, thrushes and robins I've got a pair of grey wagtails who are nesting in the climbing hydrangea above my study window. In fact they have spurned a nest box about two feet away from their chosen site, which is now occupied by a family of great tits. These charming little birds with their bobbing tails and dressed in their smart grey, black and yellow plumage bring a welcome splash of colour to the garden. A pair of pied wagtails a close relative of the yellows and equally stunning in their black and white plumage have also appeared. Between their black cap and bib is a white mask that gives these little birds an air of mystery. They are nesting on the south facing side of the house, but I've been unable, as yet, to locate their nest. They are very clever at concealing their nest site and their patience is far greater than mine. I occasionally watch them as they hunt over the roof and collect a beak full of flies. They know I am there and they will never approach their nest whilst I am watching and it is always yours truly who has to give in first and turn away, none the wiser after a seemingly long vigil.

Nuthatches are nesting in a hole in the weeping willow and I'm keeping a watchful eye on them. They nested there last year and sadly, despite their carefully selected nest hole, a grey squirrel discovered their chicks and one by one removed them all. Tawny owls are a daily site by the crossroads in the track. I suspect that they too have many mouths to feed and are extending their working hours to suit.

I keep a daily watch for the return of the spotted fly-catchers. They are one of the last summer migrants to arrive in this country because they must be sure of finding a plentiful supply of food awaiting them when they get here. They still haven't arrived and obviously have no knowledge of the unnaturally warm start to the year.

Perhaps someone should have told them!

August

As I sit and write this we are really into the summer the temperature is soaring into the late twenties and nothing much is stirring in the surrounding Forest. The activity at the bird feeders has diminished slightly and consequently I don't have to replenish the food on a daily basis, but I expect that it will a short-lived respite. I regret to report that I haven't seen the spotted flycatchers this year and I don't think they'll put in an appearance this late in the season. It's the first time since I've lived here that I haven't had the privilege of watching them flitting up and down from the top wire of the fence to catch the bounty of flies for their hungry brood. I'm also missing the nightjars; these mysterious night-fliers could always be seen at dusk hawking over the trees on the boundary of the paddocks. I've watched for them for some time but to no avail, I wonder what has happened to them, and hope that I will see them next year.

I noticed, last week, as I was cutting the lawn, a pair of swallows working in the air space above the garden. Nothing much to get excited about I hear you say, but it is to me, for swallows, martins and swifts are very seldom sighted up here and I have been trying to encourage them on the house by fixing imitation nests under the eaves, but with no success. There are old nest scars on the building and I imagine that one of my predecessors had washed or knocked them down and thus discouraged the return of the builders. I know they make a bit of a mess, but I think it's a privilege to share ones home with these little birds that have flown all the way from Africa in order to hatch and rear their young. So it was with interest that I stopped the mower and watched the darting pair. To my delight, one after the other they suddenly swooped down and into the stable through the top half of the open door and they didn't reappear. I crept closer the stable block and could see the pair perched side by side on the steel bars that separate the loose boxes. They were both excitedly twittering and seemed to be inspecting a prospective home and why not? It's a nice dry building with plenty of beams and ledges and a good supply of nest building mud at the margins of the pond, just the place for any self respecting swallow. They've been around now for several days and are continually inspecting the stable, there's no sign of a nest as yet, but there's still time.

The swallows were not my only surprise that day. I continued with my grass cutting and as I drove past the pond I glanced down at the water and to my astonishment saw dozens of tadpoles wriggling in the deep end. I couldn't believe my eyes. The pond was created about six years ago and since then I have tried repeatedly and unsuccessfully to encourage frogs and toads to take up residence. I was delighted therefore to see this swarming mass of tadpoles but I don't ever recall seeing them this late in the year. If the grass snakes and herons give them a chance I might be lucky and see some more spawn next year.

On Sunday I was sitting on the patio reading a book and soaking up the sun when a movement on the low brick wall caught my attention. In the shadow cast by a garden chair I could see something clinging to the wall, and then it moved and to my delight I could see that it was a common lizard. I watched it for many minutes as it ran quickly across the baking brickwork from shade to shade. I've often seen them in the stable yard but never this close to the house. I've also got crows. A pair of carrion crows have been frequent visitors over the years and this season they have reared two chicks that are now indistinguishable from the parent birds. Indistinguishable that is until they land on the lawn to feed and then the difference is obvious, for despite the fact that we are in July and that the chicks are quite capable of looking after themselves the parent birds are still feeding them. I'm frequently woken at some unearthly hour to the sound of raucous caws from the youngsters as they beg food from their parents.

If they don't go soon I'll give them something to crow about!

September

Summer is still with us but there is a hint of autumn in the early mornings and late evenings. The bird song is almost non existent apart from the occasional robin; he doesn't sing at this time of the year to attract a mate but to warn others that this is his territory.
Swallows are starting to gather on the wires, a sure sign that summer is coming to an end, and if you are wondering, no, they didn't nest in my stables after all, but I like to think that they've earmarked the site for next year.
The blackberries are turning and I've already had my first taste of blackberry and apple pie, a combination of flavours that must have

been invented in heaven. The sweet chestnut, hazel nut and acorn crops look promising but I have been unable (u p   h e r e, anyway) to find any evidence of a beech mast crop. Perhaps they had such a bumper h a r v e s t   l a s t autumn that the trees do not feel the   need   to reproduce   this year.

Red Kite

For those of you who are interested in Forest fungi look out for Chantrelle, Hedgehogs, Giant puffballs and Oyster mushrooms. The warm weather combined with the good rain showers that we've had recently has promoted some early growth. Please remember, do not pick anything you are unsure of and don't be greedy and pick more than the recommended personal limit of 1.5 kg. I was listening to the local radio recently and I heard a report of two sightings of red kites near the Forest. One sighting was at Ringwood and the other was close to Totton. These are magnificent birds and are becoming very common, thanks to successful release programmes, in other parts of the country but my nearest personal sighting was, until recently, near Hungerford. Imagine my delight when, as I was driving across the ridge on the B3078 near Deadman Hill, I spotted my first red kite on the Forest. I'm sure that other motorists must have thought me mad as I hastily pulled over and jumped out of the car with my binoculars. Keep your eyes peeled for a sight of these birds, they are generally bigger than a buzzard and if you cannot see their beautiful red plumage that gives them their name, then look for the distinctive forked tail that will enable you to distinguish it from other large birds of prey. Incidentally, the child's toy kite was named after these birds because of their habit of hovering in the sky.

I was blessed not long after the aforementioned sighting with the most incredible appearance of a family group of three peregrine falcons. I was fishing at Damerham when they passed over the lakes chattering shrilly to each other and giving me a very privileged view of them. Not long after that I saw another single peregrine just by the Crow fork at Burley Street, so keep a look out for these sleek falcons as you move around the Forest.

Whilst at the New Forest show I mentioned the presence of these birds to one of the men on the RSPB stand. He told me that the red kite was probably an offspring from birds that were released near Basingstoke some three years ago. He informed me that peregrines had nested this year on one of the Fawley power station chimneys, the Sway tower and Salisbury cathedral spire and he reckoned that these nesting sites could have been the source of the birds I had spotted. Finally listen out in the early morning and at dusk for the owls. It's that time of year when they are very vocal and it's entertaining to sit out and listen to the many and varied noises they make as they talk to each other. But if you don't they won't give a hoot!

November

Let me tell you about my moles. When I purchased this unique property back in 1994 the lawns were a mess. There were mole hills everywhere, it was impossible to contemplate grass cutting without first laboriously removing the piles of soil with a wheelbarrow and shovel. Without doubt they had to go, but I had no idea of how to rid the garden of moles so I decided to seek some advice.

Garden Snail

A wise old Keeper told me to buy some traps. A less informed relation pooh-poohed the Keepers advice "A waste of time, they don't work. Get some mole fuses." He instructed. The mole fuses were tracked down and purchased, the instructions were carefully followed and the fizzing charges were placed in the mole runs. Did they work? - They did not, and several newly formed mole hills were proof of their failure.

"Get some traps." said the Keeper, when I told my tale. Now in truth, I was about to buy some traps as instructed, when the ancient pipe that ran underground from the oil tank to the boiler gave up the ghost and burst. Fortunately, the tank was low and due to be refilled in the next day or so, but nevertheless several gallons of expensive heating oil percolated through the subsoil and into the well. The burst pipe and a restock of oil were easily resolved, but what to do with all the oily water in my well? A wicked idea came to mind and I could almost feel little devil horns sprouting from my temples as I contemplated the ravaged lawn, but I pushed my conscience behind me and fetched a pump. I pushed the delivery hose into the nearest mole run dropped the suction hose in the well and started the engine. Within minutes little fountains of water began to appear all over the lawn – surely that would drive them out. No, you're right, it didn't. It took days to rid the garden of the smell of oil, and the moles? Well they just shrugged off their diving bottles and carried on heaping the soil, as moles do.

Mint Beetle

"Get some traps" said the Keeper. I was about to follow his advice when Bob the handy man arrived in his old van. "Going to smoke 'em out" he explained as he connected one end of a length of hose to the exhaust pipe of the vehicle and shoved the other end in the mole run. He started the engine and we waited. After an hour or so it was difficult to see from one side of the lawn to the other - a thick pea-souper of exhaust fumes hovered above the lawn. "That should do it" he said as he disconnected the pipes and departed. No, (you've got the general idea by now, haven't you?) it didn't.

The moles, untroubled by the attack, removed their gas masks and continued to reshape my little part of the Forest.

"I've told you, - get some traps" barked the Keeper. At that moment my relation, (yes, he of the mole fuse episode) arrived armed with a dozen or so toy windmills; you'll know them, a length of cane with four plastic veins on the top.

"Just read somewhere that if you stick these in the lawn the vibrations from the windmill going round will travel down the cane and drive the moles away" He explained. The Keeper glared at him and said something that I cannot repeat and took his leave. We stuck the windmills in the lawn and when finished, it resembled a mini wind farm and then we waited. The dogs didn't wait however, they soon found them; they plucked them from the ground and charged around the garden with the windmills spinning from their mouths. Needless to say these frail toys did not survive for long but the moles did. Then one morning, soon after, I had just stepped out of the shower when I noticed that one of the moles was actually working and the hill under which he was digging was growing at an incredible rate. Without further ado I threw a towel around my waist, some slippers on my feet and tucked a shotgun under my arm. I crept up to the rapidly expanding mole hill and prepared to blast it. No, I didn't shoot the mole, and I didn't really expect to. It had detected my approach and 'done a runner' or whatever moles do, but the loosely attached towel did fall off and left me exposed, clad only in a shotgun and a pair of carpet slippers. So, you can guess what I did, after that is, donning some more suitable clothing, I went and bought some traps and with some help from my friend the Keeper I caught four moles in no time at all and thus solved my problem. Over the years I have caught many more moles for others by this method, which just goes to show that it pays to take counsel from those who should know.

Keep your Keeper sweet!

December

The New Forest is our newest National Park and is noted for its many diverse habitats, not least of which are its rare wetlands which are considered to be some of the most important in Europe. In order to create more sites for conifer plantations and to improve grazing for stock, large areas of bog woodland and wetlands were destroyed in the late 1800's and again in the 1950's. Mires were drained and watercourses were dredged and straightened in order to increase the flow velocity in the rivers and as a result reduced the seasonal flooding. In subsequent years this foolhardy action has resulted in severe erosion of the river banks together with headward erosion of untouched, upstream reaches; and the reduction in seasonal flooding has meant that many hectares of riverine and bog woodland together with valley mires and grass wetlands have been deprived or destroyed. The effects on rare and unique species of plants, invertebrates and birds have been severe but hopefully recoverable. After much consultation with the many concerned organisations, in 2002 the LIFE 3 project was launched to restore some of these diminished habitats. The project is co-ordinated by Hampshire County Council and forty percent of the estimated cost of £2.9 million is being provided by the European Union from its LIFE Nature programme. The remaining 60 percent is provided by the other LIFE 3 partners who are the RSPB, the Forestry Commission, English Nature, the National trust and the Environment Agency.

It was decided that certain actions were required to rectify the situation and these included raising river bed levels, the reinstatement of old meanders and the installation of debris dams, which hopefully would result in much slower watercourses, which once again, would have the ability to overflow onto the adjacent flood plains. Prior to the restoration work extensive surveys were carried out by the various bodies to establish, among other things, the locations of the old river courses before the modifications took place; the existing population of invertebrates and fish; and similarly a count of the numbers of the resident wetland birds such as curlew and snipe. These surveys will continue during and beyond the completion of the project in order to monitor the effects of the restoration works.

Before work could start on the modifications to the watercourses it was necessary for the Forestry Commission operatives to remove some non-native species such as rhododendron and hemlock that had, over the years, invaded the area. At the same time, some pollarding and coppicing of holly, oak and beech and the removal of scrub was also undertaken. Immediately before the commencement of work on each stretch of water, the Environment Agency operatives electro-fished for and caught and removed the resident fish stocks. A low voltage electrical rod was used to stun the fish before they were removed and relocated upstream of the work site. Heather bales, harvested from the forest were then placed across the river beds to create a temporary obstacle to their return.

Because of the boggy nature of the ground the use of specialised equipment such as tracked dumpers and excavators was essential. The watercourses that had previously been dredged were infilled with thousands of tons of hoggin (a mixture of gravel and clay), some of which had been hauled from other restoration work sites or had been imported from locally approved suppliers. The hoggin when compacted in the river will seal the bed and prevent any water loss through this route; the clay content of the upper ten centimetres or so, will, however, be quickly washed away leaving clean gravel redds for the spawning sea trout that are regular migrants to the forest streams. Wherever it was possible to identify the route of the original watercourses they were reinstated and in addition, further meanders were created to increase the length of the rivers by some thirty to forty percent. Ten metre long clay plugs were installed, where necessary, to prevent the river returning to its previous artificial route and in addition, backwaters were created to provide still-water sanctuaries for migrating fish and breeding invertebrates. Culverts, which have an eroding effect on the river bed immediately downstream, had been installed under forest tracks and by-ways. These were removed and to enable the passage of vehicles and stock, were replaced by shallow fords.

The project will come to a close in 2006 and it is anticipated that by then more than 600 acres of rare and vulnerable wetland will have been restored. Further more, conditions and contingencies will have been established to ensure their continued natural regeneration and sustainability.   These re-established habitats will not only be beneficial to many rare, unique and endangered species, they will also help to reduce the flooding to properties downstream by holding the water, at times of high rain fall, back on the natural flood-plains which will consequently, in time, provide additional grazing for forest stock.

Have an enjoyable Christmas and New Year

Ian Thew

The other books From a New Forest Inclosure

From a New Forest Inclosure
The First Two Years
Ian Thew

From a New Forest Inclosure
Book Two 2006 & 2007
Ian Tew

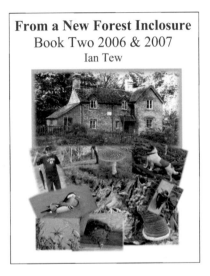

From a New Forest Inclosure
Book Three 2008 & 2009
Ian Thew

From a New Forest Inclosure
Book Four 2010 & 2011
Ian Thew

These books are available by post: Please send £5,99 per book plus £2.50 postage and packaging (up to four books) to Ian Thew, Burley Rails Cottage, Burley BH24 4HT England Or telephone 01425 403735 with your name, postal address and card details. Email ian@ithew.freeserve.co.uk

Burley Rails Cottage, Wilfs Cabin and Paddocks

Wilfs Cabin

Stables

Wilfs Cabin; a self-contained, snug, traditional log cabin that provides a double bed room with en-suite shower, a cosy lounge and a galley kitchen. The timbered veranda is ideal for alfresco dining or for just relaxing with a glass of wine after a busy day in the Forest.

For the four legged visitors there are two, modern, block-built, stables with individual yards and a tack room with all facilities, which are adjacent to two small turn-out paddocks. There is ample parking and undercover storage for traps and bikes.

www.burleyrailscottage.co.uk   Tel:01425 403735

Well behaved and sociable dogs are also welcome.